MW00604672

Illustrations prepared in coordination with Kate Armstrong, Bella Mi Design Boutique.

ISBN 978-0-98215-991-0

Gnaana Company, LLC
P.O. Box 37635 #13525
Philadelphia, PA 19101

www.gnaana.com

Bindi Baby

gnaana

जानवर • Jaanvar

Animals (Hindi)

स

सुअर

suar

ब

बतख

batakh

ह

हाथी

haathee

म

मेंढक

mEndak

बाघ

baagh

क

कुत्ता

kuttaa

ਤ

उल्लू

ulloo

घ

घोड़ा

ghorDaa

म

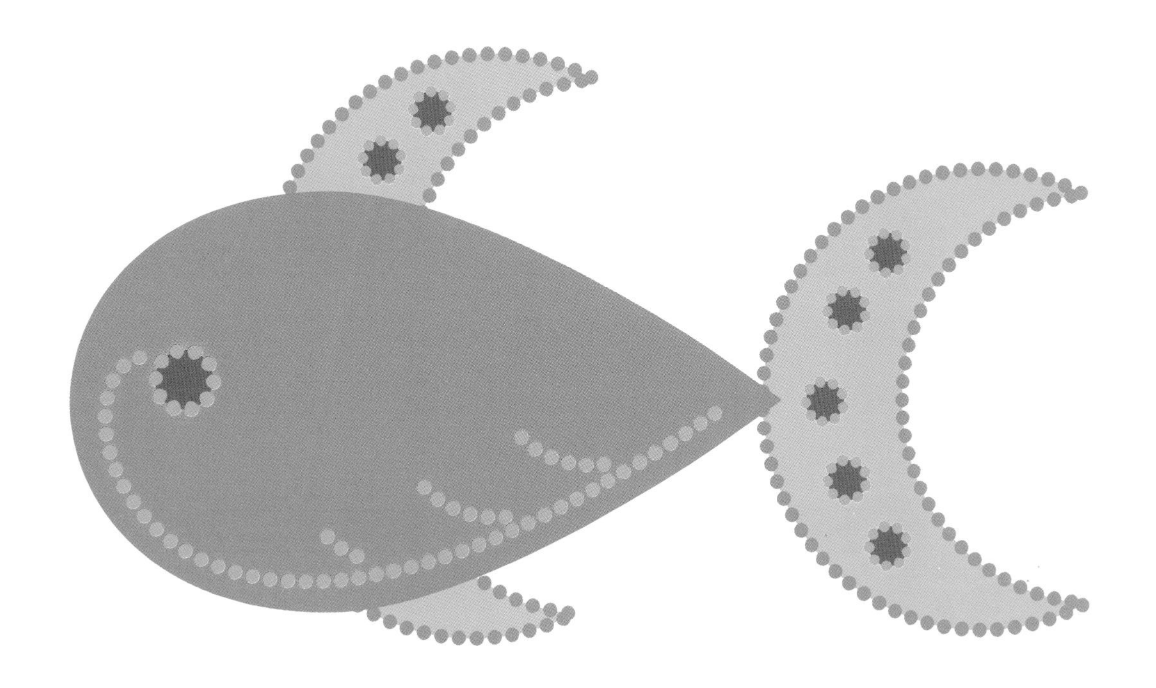

मछली

maChlee

स

साँप
saamp

ह

हिरन

hiran

प

पक्षी

pakShee

म

मोर
mor

ग

गाय

gaay

बंदर

bandar

च

चूहा

choohaa

ब

बिल्ली

billee

ख

ख़रगोश

khargosh

श

शेर
shEr

क

कछुआ

kaChuaa

HINDI

अ आ इ ई उ ऊ ऋ

a aa i ee u oo Ri

ए ऐ ओ औ अं अः

E ai o ou an aha

क ख ग घ ङ

ka kha ga gha nga

च छ ज झ ञ

cha Cha ja jha nya

ट ठ ड ढ ण

Ta Tha Da Dha Na

त थ द ध न

ta tha da dha na

प फ ब भ म

pa pha ba bha ma

य र ल व श ष

ya ra la va sha Sha

स ह क्ष त्र ज्ञ

sa ha kSha tra gnya

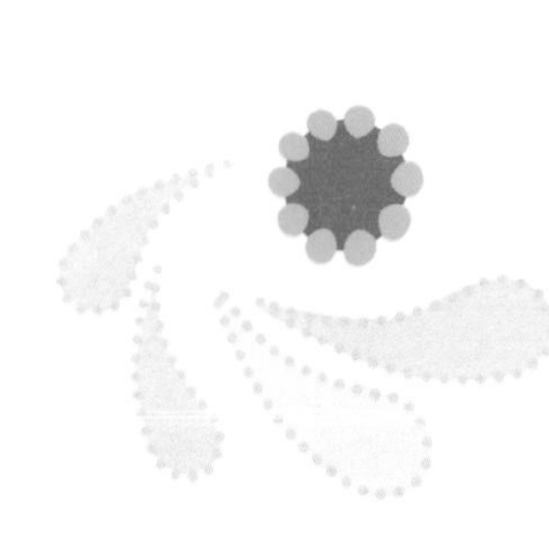

Made in the USA
San Bernardino, CA
20 March 2014